A QUICK HISTORY OF THE UNIVERSE

A QUICK HISTORY OF THE UNIVERSE

FROM THE BIG BANG TO JUST NOW

Clive Gifford and Rob Flowers

WIDE EYED EDITIONS

CONTENTS

INTRODUCTION

This book is the story of **EVERYTHING**.

You see, there's big, really **BIG**, and then there's the Universe.

The Universe is everything we know about (and quite a few things we don't). It's all the stars, planets, moons, galaxies, comets, dust, gas, and the **BIG**, **BIG**, **BIG** areas of space in between.

The Universe includes absolutely everything you can experience with your senses. In other words, it's all the things you can see, hear, taste, touch, and smell—as well as all the things you'd rather not.

It's also all the mysterious invisible forces and energies that whizz things around, makes things go **BANG**, and hold some things together while dragging other things **APART**. Oh, and did I mention that among the Universe's contents list is **TIME** itself?

I MIGHT BE IN THERE SOMEWHERE, TOO!

To understand the Universe, it helps to know its history, which scientists believe began about 13.8 billion years ago. This book tells the story of its incredible journey from as next to nothing as you can get... to **EVERYTHING** you can possibly imagine.

Along the way you'll learn about the biggest ever **EXPLOSIONS**, about the time before time itself and whether or not aliens exist.*

Get ready for an incredible journey through time and space!

LET'S GO!

*OK, full disclosure, we don't know the answer to that for sure yet. But we'll see how likely it is, anyway.

IN THE BEGINNING

In the beginning, there wasn't really anything...

It wasn't exactly that there was **NOTHING** but everything in the whole of the Universe was **SQUEEZED UP** into a point infinitely smaller than what you could see with the naked eye.

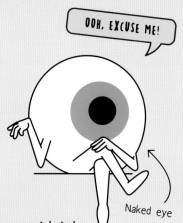

Naked eye

I don't know about you, but if I look in the fridge for a midnight snack and the thing in there is infinitely smaller than I can see, I think it's reasonable to complain that there's **NOTHING** for me to eat.

We're talking millions and millions of times smaller than the full stop ending this sentence.

Everything, **ABSOLUTELY EVERYTHING** that makes up the Universe, including space, time, and energy, was all squeezed into this infinitely tiny point. Then, something incredible, wondrous, and dramatic happened…

Everything started spreading outward a gazillion* times *faster* than you can possibly imagine.

We call this the **'BIG BANG'** although the name's a bit confusing.

You see, big-brained scientists don't think it was a regular explosion like those caused by bombs or sticks of dynamite. All we know is that the Universe began e x p a n d i n g at an incredible rate.

But we do think it was the beginning… the very beginning… of the Universe.

I THINK WE SHOULD CALL IT "THE BIG AND EXTREMELY RAPID OUTWARD EXPANSION OF MATTER AND ENERGY."

MMM… CATCHY!

*OK, OK, a gazillion isn't very scientific, but it's the idea of an incredibly large number.

BLINK OF AN EYE

The very first moments of the Universe remain unknown to us. **?**
We call this microscopically ᵗⁱⁿʸ tiny fraction of a second of the Universe's
existence the **PLANCK ERA,** after a famous physicist, **MAX PLANCK.**

The **PLANCK ERA** was so short that you'd need 550,000 trillion trillion
trillion of them in a row just for you to blink your eye.

Scientists believe that the normal
laws of physics didn't apply
during the **PLANCK ERA**. What
was actually going on, however,
is a total, utter mystery… a bit like
why the word "abbreviation" is so
long, or where all your
odd socks disappear to…
only it's a far bigger puzzler!

After the **PLANCK ERA**, the Universe was extremely hot, dense, and more energetic than a lively PE teacher after a sugar rush. For an incredibly short period, the Universe iNFLATED at a mind-numbing rate. In less than a trillionth of a second, we think it grew from 10,000 times smaller than an atom to about the size of a grapefruit.

After a millionth of a second, the Universe may have ballooned to the size of our solar system (read more about our solar system from page 68). At that point, the Universe had cooled down a lot, but was still beyond red hot, at **10,000 MILLION DEGREES**. And to think we consider 95 °F (35 °C) a pretty hot summer's day!

But more changes were to come by the time the Universe celebrated its first birth-second.

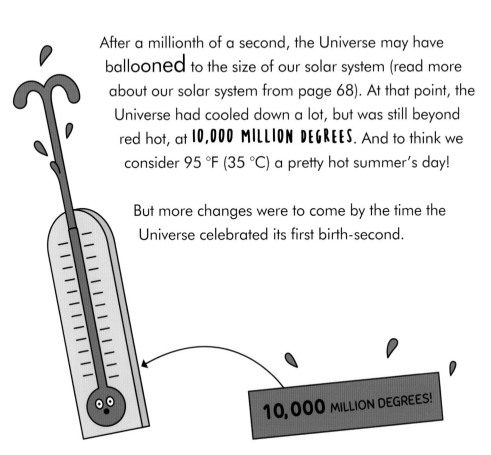

10,000 MILLION DEGREES!

free electrons

THE FIRST SECONDS

After one second, the Universe had **GROWN** to around a thousand times the size of our solar system. It had also cooled further, possibly down to "just" **1,000** MILLION DEGREES. Not exactly chilly, eh?

If the rapid growth and ridiculously hot temperatures weren't enough, things got kinda **FUNKY** and F R E A K Y. Although, you wouldn't have been able to see just how weird it all was, as the Universe was full of free electrons.

I'M FREE!

These tiny particles got in the way of light traveling. And light traveling between objects and our eyes is how we see things. So, if light cannot travel, you cannot see anything. (Not that you or your ancestors, or indeed anything at all, were around just after the Big Bang to do much sightseeing.)

I CAN'T WAIT TO SHOW EYE THIS FLOWER.

light traveling between an object and our eye is how we see stuff

EYE'S GONNA **LOVE** IT!

But just because things couldn't be seen, doesn't mean that there wasn't **STUFF** going on. And my, was there **STUFF** going on.

A cosmic "soup" built up incredibly rapidly. It contained electrons and other elementary particles such as quarks and antiquarks. These were among the first particles produced in the **BIG BANG**, back within its first millionth of a second. Scientists think there are six types of quark, which they call **UP**, **DOWN**, **TOP**, **BOTTOM**, **STRANGE**, and **CHARM**.

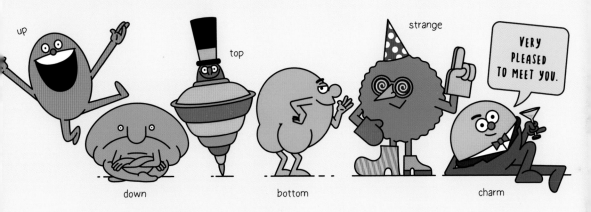

up

top

strange

VERY PLEASED TO MEET YOU.

down

bottom

charm

Quarks quickly formed other particles such as protons and neutrons. You might not have heard of **PROTONS** and **NEUTRONS**, but you may have heard of **ATOMS**. Atoms themselves are made of other particles like **PROTONS**, **NEUTRONS**, and **ELECTRONS**. These tiny building blocks make up every physical thing in the Universe.

The story of atoms is l o n g, with plenty of action and more **BREAK - UPS** and **SPL ITS** than a romantic movie and it sort of starts about **NOW**.

Meet the atom

UHH, YEAH, I'M KINDA LIKE A **BIG DEAL**, ACTUALLY. I'M FOUND IN LIKE **EVERYTHING**.

WHAT'S THE MATTER?

Matter is **STUFF**. It's all the **STUFF** around us—from this book to a tennis ball or your fingernail. Matter can vary in size from the most microscopic mould found in your stinky trainers to the biggest airliner, skyscraper, planet, or star.

The very, very early Universe lacked matter that you would recognize—not tennis balls and **DEFINITELY** not fingernails—but it did have the particles that would eventually form atoms.

Atoms are incredibly tiny. Your fingernail measures around 100 million atoms in width.

A SINGLE NAIL IS AROUND 100 MILLION ATOMS WIDE.

All matter is made up of atoms. Each atom's a collection of **PROTONS** and **NEUTRONS** in its center, called a nucleus, with one or more **ELECTRONS** sort of flying or orbiting around the nucleus.

I FEEL SO EMPTY INSIDE.

MORE THAN 99.99% OF EVERY ATOM IS EMPTY SPACE!

An **ATOM** usually has the same numbers of **ELECTRONS** as it does **PROTONS**. Different chemical elements (more on those in a mo) have different numbers of these particles. So, a helium atom, for instance, has two electrons, two protons, and two neutrons, while a carbon atom has six of each (plus six neutrons in its center).

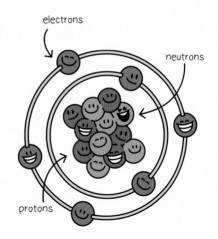

electrons

neutrons

protons

Speaking of chemical elements, we now know of 118 different ones; 92 are found naturally, with the others created in labs by scientists. They range from heavy, soft metals like **lead** to light gases like oxygen and helium. Hydrogen is the lightest of all.

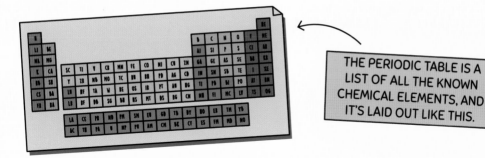

THE PERIODIC TABLE IS A LIST OF ALL THE KNOWN CHEMICAL ELEMENTS, AND IT'S LAID OUT LIKE THIS.

In the first few minutes after the **BIG BANG**, temperatures cooled enough for neutrons and protons to get it together. They grabbed dance partners to form the first nuclei of atoms. Yay! They weren't complete atoms, but they were on their way.

Scientists call this the **ERA OF NUCLEOSYNTHESIS**, but as eras go, it didn't last long.

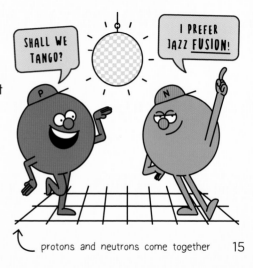

SHALL WE TANGO?

I PREFER JAZZ FUSION!

protons and neutrons come together   15

GET ATOM!

There were no slow, long dances in the **ERA OF NUCLEOSYNTHESIS**. The whole thing was all over within 20 minutes of the **BIG BANG**. Whoosh!

Many **PROTONS** were left on the dance floor alone, having failed to partner up with neutrons, but they didn't mind. Protons have a **POSITIVE** electrical charge, so they always look on the bright side. (Science disclaimer: having a positive charge is nothing to do with moods—protons don't have moods).

> WITHOUT A PARTNER, I CAN DANCE HOWEVER I LIKE!

And there was another upside to not partnering with any neutrons. You see, one chemical element plays by slightly different rules to those I mentioned before, and has no neutrons in its nucleus. That element is hydrogen, which is the most abundant element in the Universe.

> I JUST DON'T PLAY BY THE RULES.

So, a proton on its lonesome is an entire nucleus of a hydrogen atom all by itself. No neutron necessary.

By the end of the all-too-brief **ERA OF NUCLEOSYNTHESIS**, vast numbers of these lone protons, along with lots of nuclei of helium atoms,* could be found in the fog of the very early Universe.

All these nuclei needed to do in order to become entire atoms was to attract electrons. Sounds straightforward as there were LOTS of free electrons around. And electrons with their **NEGATIVE** electrical charge are attracted to protons.

But the Universe was still so hot, hot, hot, that the different particles kept bouncing off each other. They simply had too much energy to settle down and form **ATOMIC RELATIONSHIPS**.

YOU COMPLETE ME!

The Universe needed to grow up↑ and cool down↓ before atoms could form.

OVER HERE!

COME AND JOIN ME!

*There were also very small amounts of other, lighter, chemical elements, such as lithium.

GETTING BIGGER

While protons and neutrons were clubbing together, the Universe was still expanding. After 10 seconds, it had stretched to about 100 light years across—roughly the same as 20 trips from Earth to the next nearest star (after the Sun), Proxima Centauri.

MY, HOW YOU'VE GROWN!

AFTER 20 MINUTES, IT WAS AROUND 3,000 LIGHT YEARS IN SIZE.

Just to highlight how **BIG** a light year is, to walk one light year (at a typical speed of 3 mph) would take you over 215 million years! And all without rest stops, sleeps, or toilet breaks. So, as things go or indeed gr**OW** (ahem), the Universe was a rapid developer (read more about light years on pages 105–106).

The Universe continued to get **BIGGER** and **BIGGER** in all directions and still does to this day. But it doesn't expand quite in the way you normally think of things getting larger. You know, like your dad's waistline or a cartoon snowball rolling down a slope.

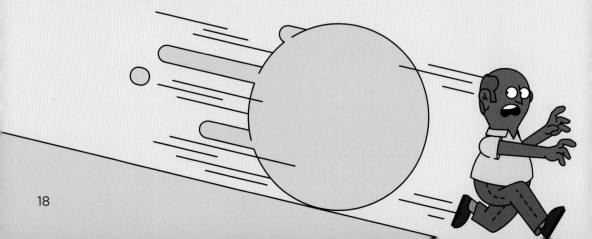

The Universe isn't expanding into anything. After all, the Universe is **EVERYTHING**, so how could it expand into something else? It is actually space itself that is expanding... Mindnumbing, isn't it?

It might help if you think of the **UNIVERSE** like a balloon, with little spots stuck to its surface acting as matter. When the balloon is blown up a little, the space between the spots increases. Blow it up more and the space increases again.

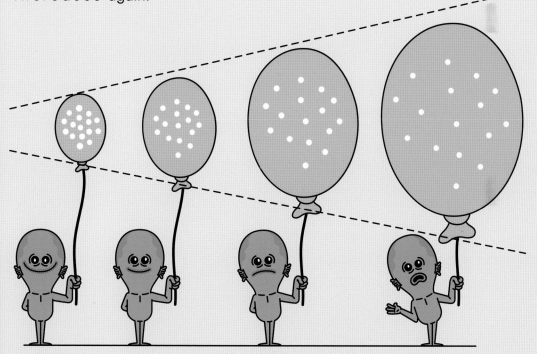

Such was the case with the Universe, which expanded to millions of light years in diameter in a relatively short time (less than 300,000 years).

And speaking of time...

TIME FOR TIME

Every day, you use "**BEFORE**" and "**AFTER**," "**PAST**," "**PRESENT**," and "**FUTURE**" to describe moments in time. So, try to imagine a time *before* time. Confusing, innit?

You see, most scientists talk of there being no "before the Big Bang," because time did not exist. **TIME**, just like space and energy, began during the Big Bang and has continued ever since.

Unlike matter, which has **THREE DIMENSIONS** (height, width, and depth), time has only one. It continues in one direction → forward → . As far as we can tell, there's no way of stopping time. Nor, can you turn back time… sorry, wannabe time travelers.

You can slow the effects of time on objects moving really close to the *speed of light*. This mind-numbing idea was made popular by **ALBERT EINSTEIN**—the 20th century's number **ONE** celeb science genius. It's called time dilation and it means that time travels more slowly when you're moving outrageously fast—close to the speed of light.

If you went on a wild space trip orbiting the fringes of a black hole without falling in (read about black holes on pages 62–63), you'd find that time passed more slowly for you. When you return to Earth, a year older, all your friends would be fully grown up.

I CAN'T BELIEVE YOU ALL WENT TO SEE FROZEN 7 WITHOUT ME.

Speaking of time, let's turn it back a little, back to the first teensy fraction of a second after the Big Bang, when **ALL** the important forces that influence how objects behave were **ALL** as one.

FEEL THE FORCE

Four fundamental forces emerged moments after the **BIG BANG** to rule the Universe and no, neither the police force nor muscly superheroes were among them.

HERE ARE THE FAB FOUR.

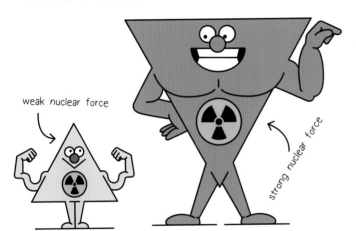

weak nuclear force

strong nuclear force

The **STRONG NUCLEAR FORCE** binds protons and neutrons together at the center of atoms. This force is powerful but only acts inside atoms so it works over a very, very, very short distance.

The **WEAK NUCLEAR FORCE** also only works inside atoms. It causes some atomic particles to change and can cause atoms to decay and produce **RADIOACTIVITY**.

All particles with an electric charge, such as electrons and protons, are affected by **ELECTROMAGNETISM**. It's a big deal, holding atoms and molecules (collections of atoms) together and generating **LIGHT** (see p30–31) and other electromagnetic radiation like radio waves. It's also behind magnetic and electric fields, which we have learned to harness to generate super-useful **ELECTRICITY**.

GRAVITY is a pulling force of attraction between objects. It's so important to know about when looking at the Universe that it has its very own double page (overleaf). Don't tell the other three—they might get jealous.

Straight after the **BIG BANG**, scientists think all four forces were all squashed together because of the Universe's outrageously extreme temperatures and densities.

But in the first fractions of that first second, the four forces separated out. Scientists think that the first to bail was the force that holds us and the Universe all together… **gravity**.

A MATTER OF GRAVITY

Gravity is the **PULLING FORCE** of attraction between different objects. It's invisible, but its effects can be seen all around you. Just throw a ball up...

All matter exerts some gravity, but the more matter something has, the greater its gravity. That means **REALLY MASSIVE** objects like planets and stars have seriously noticeable pulling power. Earth's own gravity, for example, holds its gassy atmosphere in place. Without it, the atmosphere would drift away. By-eeee!

English scientist **ISAAC NEWTON** was the first to identify and understand parts of this fabulous force in the 17th century after an apple fell on his head. (Allegedly. It was a long time ago). He figured out that **gravity** works across space, but gets weaker the farther a p a r t objects are.

That said, gravity, unlike the weak and strong nuclear forces, can work over TRULY VAST distances, binding stars together in large collections called galaxies even though they are many light years apart.

Objects orbit around other, more massive, objects, due to gravity, which pulls them into a circular or oval-shaped path through space. The planet Neptune is 2.8 billion miles from the Sun (30 times farther away than Earth), but it stays in orbit around our star due to the Sun's powerful **gravity**.

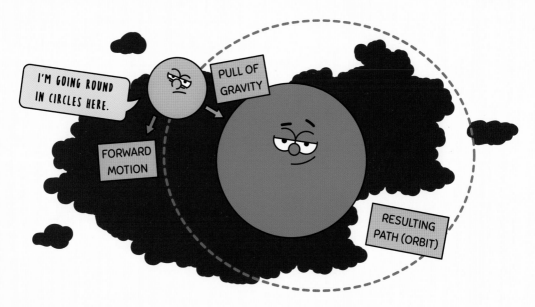

In the Universe's early days there were no planets or galaxies for gravity to work with. Gravity, though, would play a major part in bringing enough dust and gas together to form the FIRST STARS, which lit up the Universe. But that was in the future, though first the Universe had some obstacles to overcome before it could see the light.

PHOTON BOOTH

The **BIG BANG** resulted in trillions and trillions of teeny packets of energy known as **PHOTONS**. They dominated the energy of the Universe, starting around 10 seconds after the Big Bang and lasting for thousands of years—a period called the **PHOTON EPOCH**.

Photons are **FUNKY**. They wouldn't trouble even the smallest set of scales (scientists say they have zero mass). Nor do they have an electric charge like electrons. But they carry energy as they whizz through space and there are an awful lot of them.

In 2018, long after the **PHOTON EPOCH**, American scientists announced that they had worked out how many photons there are in the Universe. Have a guess... Bet you're not even close!*

*The total number of photons is: 4,000,000,000,000,000,000,000,000,000,000,000,000,000,000,000,000,000,000,000,000,000,000,000,000,000.

Photons make up the light you can see (called visible light), but that's not all. Photons also form other types of radiation, each with their own levels of energy. Together, they and visible light are known as the **ELECTROMAGNETIC SPECTRUM**. All of these are made up of photons, travel in wave-like patterns, and, if nothing's in their way, race along at the speed of light:

I'M VIOLET AND VIOLENT!

GAMMA RAYS and **X-RAYS** are the most energetic of all.

ULTRAVIOLET UV is emitted by many stars, including the Sun.

VISIBLE LIGHT and all the colors you see are somewhere in the middle, energy-wise.

INFRARED is often given off by objects and some infrared radiation can be felt as heat.

MICROWAVES and **RADIO WAVES** are the low-energy champions of the electromagnetic spectrum.

IN A FOG

As you've already seen, there was an awful **LOT** going on in the Universe straight after the **BIG BANG**.

You might think your weekends are hectic, but they're nothing compared to the infant Universe's schedule, with photons, time, space, particles, and the forces that govern them all being created all in a few blinks of an eye. You've got to admit, that's quite a serious "to-do" list.

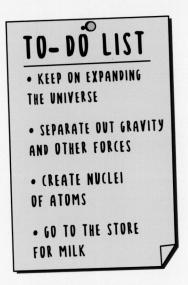

TO-DO LIST

• KEEP ON EXPANDING THE UNIVERSE

• SEPARATE OUT GRAVITY AND OTHER FORCES

• CREATE NUCLEI OF ATOMS

• GO TO THE STORE FOR MILK

But all the amazing stuff that was happening was not viewable, not yet... and wouldn't be for thousands of years.

← remember these guys from page 10?

The problem was those pesky free electrons roaming around and getting in the way of photons all of the time.

When traveling through empty space, streams of photons can whizz along at the *speed of light*. Considering some of these **are** light, that makes sense!

But in the early Universe, every time poor photons tried to move, they found themselves quickly trapped by free electrons.

A photon would bounce off one electron, move away in a different direction only to bounce off yet another electron. This process is called SCATTERING, and it stopped photons from traveling very far at all and certainly not as a stream like the light we are able to view.

As a result, the Universe remained a hard-to-see-through fog of matter and energy until the whole shebang cooled down further.

THE UNIVERSE WILL REMAIN HOT AND FOGGY ALL OVER FOR ANOTHER 377,000 YEARS.

RECOMBINATION

Remember how electrons were just too eNeRgEtIc to settle down and form atoms with protons and neutrons? (If your mind's a little scrambled, it's back on page 19).

Well, 377,000 years after the Big Bang, the ever-expanding Universe was really on a **COOL DOWN**.

IS IT ME OR IS IT GETTING CHILLY?

HE

Its temperature, once measured in millions or billions of degrees, had dipped below about **5400 °F.**

While this is still hot enough to melt metals like iron and titanium, it was cool enough for electrons and other subatomic particles to lose energy. And just like you when you lose energy, the particles s l o w e d down.

It meant that lone protons or the nuclei of helium atoms were able to snag roving electrons.

The different particles could now join forces to become fully fledged atoms. Hurrah!

Scientists call this **RECOMBINATION**, which is a bit weird as they'd never actually combined together before. Still, no matter! The result was a Universe made up of around three-quarters hydrogen atoms, a quarter helium atoms, and a very small number of lithium atoms.

Another important result of recombination was something called **DE-COUPLING**. Electrons no longer got in the way of photons. These were now free to travel as radiation through the Universe which, at the time, was about 1/1100th the size it is today.

The Universe changed its look dramatically. Where it had been very foggy, it was now see-through. And the radiation that could now pass freely through the Universe would still be detectable over 13.7 billion years later...

COSMIC MICROWAVE BACKGROUND

I'd like to interrupt our flow now to tell you a short story about pigeon poop. The tale involves a jump of more than 13.7 billion years, from just 377,000 years after the Big Bang to just over half a century ago—**1963** to be precise.

The 1960s were a **groovy** time for music, science, and space, with people leaving Earth in rocket-powered spacecrafts to become astronauts for the first time. Many scientists were also studying the Universe from down on the ground, including two American researchers, **ARNO PENZIAS** and **ROBERT WILSON**.

The pair were working with a large American radio telescope called the **HOLMDEL HORN ANTENNA**, but were puzzled by the faint buzzing signals their telescope was gathering in.

They thought something was broken, so checked all the wiring and instruments.

They shooed pigeons out of the telescope's big horn.

They even cleaned out all of the droppings left behind by the birds (urgh!)…

…but still the signals kept on coming and seemed to come from every single direction in space.

WELL I DIDN'T THINK PIGEON POOP WAS GOING TO BE A BIG PART OF MY JOB WHEN I CHOSE TO STUDY ASTROPHYSICS.

Scientists examined those signals and discovered they were the radiation left over from recombination over 13.7 billion years earlier! During the time that had passed, its radiation had been s t r e t c h e d by the expanding Universe and cooled as a result, down to about -450 °F. This radiation was named the **COSMIC MICROWAVE BACKGROUND** (CMB).

AM I GOING MAD?

WHEREVER I GO, I THINK THERE IS A COSMIC MICROWAVE IN THE BACKGROUND.

The discovery helped prove that the Universe *did* start according to the **BIG BANG** theory, but many mysteries remained, including one particularly *dark* one…

DARK MATTER

The **COSMIC MICROWAVE BACKGROUND** means we can peer back in time to when the Universe first became transparent.

Astronomers now get to gaze and gasp at some wondrous sights in space, but some wondered if they were really seeing the **WHOLE PICTURE.**

All matter exerts gravity on other matter. But when the scientists did all the math, they found a huge amount of matter **MISSING.**

There's not enough regular matter, the type we can detect, to explain the gravity found in the Universe. Weird, huh?

So, there must be other matter that we cannot see, which exerts the rest of the gravity. This super-secret stuff has been named *dark matter* and what's more, it's thought to make up more than four-fifths of all the matter in the Universe.

MISSING

MOST OF THE STUFF IN SPACE

?

ANSWERS TO THE NAME OF DARK MATTER, IF FOUND, PLEASE RETURN TO THE UNIVERSE

REWARD GIVEN

Dark matter doesn't give out visible light, radio waves, or X-rays. But just because we cannot see or measure it directly, doesn't mean it's not there. What is dark matter? To tell you the truth, we don't know… yet. There's lots of theories, including **MACHO**s and **WIMP**s (I know, these scientists, eh?).

MACHOs (Massive Compact Halo Objects) may be large, dark objects that hang out round the edge of galaxies.

WIMPs (Weakly Interacting Massive Particles) might be incredibly tiny and number trillions of trillions. What's more, they may actually pass right through regular matter—including YOU—without any effect.

Whether a **WIMP** or **MACHO**, it was not *dark matter's* fault that the now transparent Universe was about to spend a long spell well and truly in the dark…

IN THE DARK

Need a breather after all that intense action? Luckily, the story of the Universe provides one.

If you think that the *Cosmic Dark Age* sounds like an exciting superhero movie, think again. It was actually a long, l o n g, l o n g period when there was no light, no cameras, and very little other action. Zzzzzz.

NOW SHOWING

THE **UNIVERSE** PRESENTS

THE *Cosmic*

DARK AGE

'THE DARKEST STORY EVER TOLD'

'NO STARS, BUT BOY, IT'S DARK'

And it dragged on far longer than the last lessons before the summer holidays. It began around 377,000 years after the Big Bang and lasted for over **100 MILLION** years.

Pretty much the most notable thing that happened during this time was that the Universe cooled further, from around 4900 °F to –350 °F. **BRRRR**!

During the *Cosmic Dark Age*, matter—mostly in the form of hydrogen or helium gas—was distributed fairly evenly throughout the Universe.

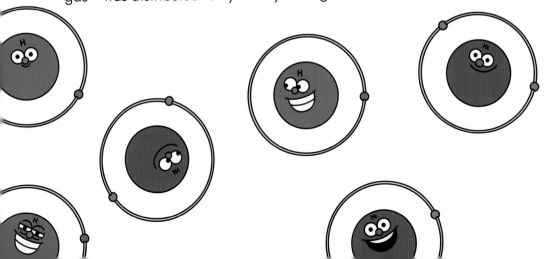

I say "fairly," as there were areas where dark matter was slightly more concentrated than elsewhere, and these areas would prove crucial to our story. Scientists think around 100–150 million years after the Big Bang, the regions with more matter in them started to shrink and collapse under their own gravity.

As the center of these shrinking clumps got more packed with matter, their **gravity** increased and they started heating up. This process didn't happen overnight, though. Many scientists reckon it took between 100,000 and 500,000 years. During this time, the clumps began to draw in even more material and start spinning round.

They had become wannabe stars, objects that we call **PROTOSTARS**. Wonder what happened next?

YOU STAR!

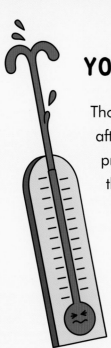

Those wannabe stars got their wish 100–200 million years after the **BIG BANG**. It all happened after each protostar's core (its middle bit) got crazy hot. When temperatures there soared above 18 million °F, something very exciting happened…

The protostar's core became an **ENORMOUS** nuclear power station—no engineers or planning permission required.

Nuclear fusion reactions in the core used hydrogen atoms as fuel. These reactions fused (joined) the hydrogen nuclei together to create helium nuclei and **HUGE** amounts of energy. No, seriously. The reactions turned protostars into STARS—giant balls of gas that shone brightly, sending out their energy into space as heat and light.

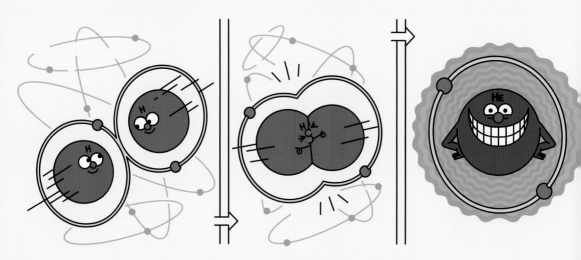

two hydrogen atoms fuse together into one helium atom

Just how much energy did they send out? Good question. Pleased you asked. We cannot measure the first stars, but scientists studying our local star (the Sun) estimate it gives out:

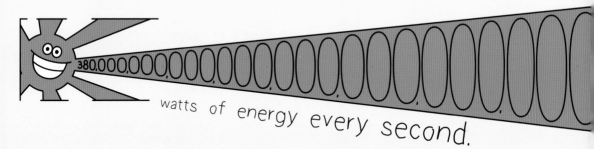

380,000,000,000,000,000,000,000,000 watts of energy every second.

Put another way, **ONE SECOND** of the Sun's total energy is more than all the energy humans have used since they first appeared on Earth. **WOW!** You get the picture.

The first ever stars were even more e N e R g E t I c than our Sun—lighting up the Universe for the first time.

I'M HERE TO LIGHT THINGS UP, BABY!

COSMIC DAWN

Who turned the lights on? The first STARS, that's who! Energy from these pioneering first **GIANT** balls of gas emitted vast amounts of energy, which lit up the early Universe.

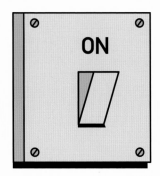

These early rise and shiners, known as Population III stars, were absolutely **MASSIVE**. Scientists estimate that even the smallest may have had 10 times the mass of the Sun, while the largest may have been 1,000 times **MORE MASSIVE**.

But these first stars didn't stick around for long. They used up their hydrogen fuel and died after just a few million years of bright, blazing glory. Sad to see them go, but they were followed by further waves of stars, and before they departed, the first stars helped do something else to the Universe.

They produced large amounts of ultra-violet (UV) light which struck the hydrogen atoms that made up most of space.

This UV light divided ÷ ded the atoms up into electrons and protons again, just like they had been shortly after the **BIG BANG**. This is called "**IONIZING**."

UV light divided the atoms into separate protons and electrons.

By the time the Universe celebrated its one billionth birthday (imagine the candles…), most of space had been ionized. What's more, lots of important new **CHEMICAL ELEMENTS** had come to the party, elements such as oxygen, iron, and silicon, all produced by the first stars and the way they ended violently.

HERE'S CARBON!

Hydrogen was the Universe's **NUMBER ONE** chemical element. But until the first stars lived and died, it only had helium to keep it company. When early stars ran out of hydrogen, they had a further trick up their sleeves (if they had had sleeves, which of course they didn't, silly me).

They started using helium as fuel, which produced **heavier** chemical elements such as **CARBON**. Hats off to carbon—without it there'd be no life as we know it. Carbon forms bonds with lots of other elements, making things like proteins, fats, carbohydrates, and other substances 100% vital to **LIFE**. Every animal—including you, me, and even your science teacher—is a carbon-based lifeform.

Then, as their fusion reactions continued, carbon and helium atoms got it together—forming atoms of oxygen. This gas is super important. You breathe it in all the time and use it to turn food into energy. It's also needed for combustion (burning) to occur.

This process went on and on with more and more elements being made...until the star's core got to iron. Now, iron was stubborn, didn't react, and refused to join the fusion party. Misery-guts!

THIS PARTY'S LAME.

I'D NEVER FUSE WITH YOU LOT.

iron wouldn't fuse with other elements

With nuclear fusion no longer an option, stars began to die. Many stars ended their lives spectacularly in EXPLOSIONS called supernovae.

This sent much of the star, including these **heavier** elements, hurtling through space only to embark on a new adventure...

TURNING CLOUDY

Those scattered elements from dying early stars mixed with hydrogen and helium in space to form **GIANT** molecular clouds of dust and gas. Scientists call these nebulae. Like a particularly lazy older brother, nebulae often just sat there, doing very little, until they were disturbed in some way such as by a passing object or an exploding star.

Nebulae do nothing unless disturbed

CLOUDY, GETTING HOTTER, WITH A CHANCE OF STARS!

Then, parts of the cloud collapsed into denser clumps with increasing gravity pulling in more and more material. The clumps' centers grew hotter and hotter and more and more dense until…can you guess?

…they formed a protostar, which later became a star. **BOOM!** Here we go again!

Only this time, these **STARS** were different. Many were much smaller and lived longer lives—billions of years long. To live long and prosper, these new stars performed quite some **BALANCING ACT**.

Nuclear fusion in their cores produced phenomenally high temperatures and energy which all pushed outward. At the same time, as **MASSIVE** objects, these stars had strong gravity, which pulled everything inward toward their cores.

I AM A VERY **BALANCED** INDIVIDUAL.

Stars balancing these forces as they perform nuclear fusion are said to be on the **MAIN SEQUENCE**. Our **SUN**, for instance, is roughly halfway along its main sequence, which will last around 10 billion years. Other stars, smaller than the Sun, may have far longer main sequences. As these stars balanced and blazed away, the first galaxies were getting it together.

our Sun is halfway through its 10 billion year lifespan

GALAXIES GET IT TOGETHER

Experts used to think the first **GALAXIES** arrived a good billion years after the Big Bang, but that figure keeps on falling as astronomers find older and older galaxies. In 2016, astronomers using the **HUBBLE SPACE TELESCOPE** discovered the oldest galaxy so far—GN-z11. It's absolutely ancient—13.4 billion years old!

YOU WEREN'T EVEN A SINGLE TWINKLING STAR WHEN I WAS BORN, LAD.

THOSE WERE THE GOOD OLD DAYS...

Whoa! I'm getting ahead of myself... sorry. A galaxy is a collection of STARS, clouds of gas, dust, and other stuff all bound together by **gravity**. Well, they are today. Astronomers think that the very first galaxies may have started forming WITHOUT stars from a build-up of *dark matter*. I know, crazy isn't it?

EARLY GALAXY

NO STARS!

The first galaxies eventually gained stars, but were extremely tiny compared to today's **GIANT** galaxies. Mind you, they still contained thousands of stars or more.

In the early Universe, some of the first galaxies collided and merged, forming bigger galaxies. Galaxies continue to collide and merge to this very day. In the future, billions of years from now, our galaxy, the **Milky Way**, is scheduled to get up close and personal to the Andromeda galaxy (see p52) and may even merge to form a **SUPER GALAXY**.

HEY, WANNA FORM A SUPER GALAXY?

Collisions, mergers, and the galaxies' gravity pulling at each other caused temperatures and pressures to rise inside some galaxies, leading to the number of new stars increasing. Over billions of years, star numbers really mounted up...

47

HOW MANY STARS?

As galaxies formed and **GALACTIC REGIONS** churned out new stars, their number **GREW** and **GREW**. On a clear night, you can spot several thousand stars (and a few night-flying aircrafts). That's nothing. Just the teensiest tip of the starry iceberg.

Most of the stars you can spot are relatively close to us and within our galaxy, the **Milky Way**. Astronomers using really **POWERFUL** telescopes can peer far further into space to discover stars in galaxies that lie **BILLIONS** of light years away.

Some stars, which first appeared as a single pinprick of light, have turned out to be **star systems**, containing two, three, or more stars. **NU SCORPII**, for instance, is a system containing seven stars.

from a distance, groups of stars can look like one single star

HEY! THERE'S SOMETHING FISHY ABOUT THAT STAR!

Our galaxy contains more than 100 billion stars. Some astronomers think it might be as high as **400 BILLION**—that's more than 50 stars for every person currently living on the planet. How big even IS a billion? Well, if you took a second to count each of the minimum 100 billion stars in the Milky Way, it would take you **3,170 YEARS 11¾ MONTHS** to count them all. Tick tock!

And the **Milky Way** is just one of the billions of galaxies that exist. Want another gobsmacking fact? There may be **10 TIMES** more stars in the observable Universe than grains of sand on Earth.

These numbers are pretty **MINDBLOWING**, aren't they? So, how do astronomers make sense of all these stars?

STAR QUALITY

Astronomers have not spotted every **STAR** in the observable Universe, but they've bagged a fair old few… more than a billion. Good work! To make sense of so many **STARS**, astronomers measure and group 'em together in different ways. Sometimes, it's by their location or distance from us.

Or it might be by their size or mass. Arcturus, for instance, has a diameter 25 times **BIGGER** than the Sun, while VY Canis Majoris is a WHOPPING 1,400 times the Sun's w i d t h.

Stars can also be lumped together by their temperature and color, known as their spectral type.

the spectral types of stars

I'M THE HOTTEST (OVER 54,000 °F)

AND APPEAR BLUE

HELLO I'M TYPE O

I'M YELLOWISH AND MY SURFACE IS 9,400–10,650 °F

HELLO I'M TYPE G

HELLO I'M TYPE M

I'M DARK RED AND THE COOLEST

(UNDER 7,000 °F)

But spare a thought for the many wannabe stars that didn't quite make it. They didn't bulk up or heat up enough to kick off those nuclear fusion reactions in their core. Awww. These failed stars, known as brown dwarfs, skulk in space, shining dimly. Some have temperatures lower than your kitchen's oven.

brown dwarfs don't bulk up enough to become real stars

In fact, our own galaxy, the Milky Way, is filled with failure. It contains around 100 billion brown dwarfs. On the plus side, the brown dwarfs have the last laugh, because—unlike successful stars which eventually burn themselves out—they never die. (The tragic death of the star is explained more on pages 58-59.) So, while life for a brown dwarf may be somewhat boring and unglamorous, at least it doesn't end!

TYPE 0
RIP

THE GALACTIC ZOO

As star numbers increased, so did galaxies. The observable Universe now has a membership of between **200** and **2,000 BILLION GALAXIES**. That's right, billion. But back in the early 1920s, people thought that only one, our **Milky Way**, existed.

It took the work of the man, the legend, **EDWIN HUBBLE**, to prove that space was full of galaxies. Before, all the fuzzy blobs spotted in the night sky were thought to be nebulae. In 1924, Hubble managed to measure the distances to stars in a nebulae called **ANDROMEDA**. They proved to be too far away to reside in the Milky Way, so Hubble concluded that Andromeda must be its own galaxy.

In 1936, Mr. Hubble was at it again with ways to group galaxies together based on their shape: ELLIPTICAL (oval-shaped), SPIRAL, BARRED SPIRAL, and IRREGULAR (having no regular shape). No wonder they named a massive telescope sent into space after him!

Galaxies have also evolved into different sizes. At 100,000 light years w i d e , the Milky Way is sort of medium-sized. Others are far smaller. Segue 2, for instance, is a mere 221 light years wide. Some are much, much **BIGGER**. For example, if Segue 2 was the size of a 500 yd by 500 yd farm field, then some of the biggest galaxies would be the size of France.

GALAXIES GANG UP

As galaxies developed, their gravity caused them to hang out with others in a posse known as a **GROUP** or a larger mob called a **CLUSTER**. Fortunately, these cosmic gangs don't steal your lunch money, as far as we know. However, they do sometimes bully the gas and dust between the galaxy members, pushing and pulling with their gravity and causing it to heat up.

The Milky Way is part of one such gang of 50 nearby* galaxies that are called the **LOCAL GROUP**. The Local Group is part of a bigger gang named the **VIRGO CLUSTER**.

Superclusters are **HUMONGOUS**. They're loose groups of clusters spread over vast areas of space. The **LANIAKEA SUPERCLUSTER**, for instance, is 520 million light years in size and is home to 100,000 galaxies. Wowzers! We're part of the **LANIAKEA SUPERCLUSTER**, so our Universal address would read:

* I say nearby, but many members of the Local Group are over 2 million light years away.

EARTH (THIRD PLANET FROM STAR)
SOLAR SYSTEM
MILKY WAY
LOCAL GROUP
VIRGO CLUSTER
LANIAKEA SUPERCLUSTER

Other superclusters include El Gordo ("the fat one" in Spanish), which is a hefty cluster, tipping the scales at a pretty **CHUNKY** 3 million billion stars! Astronomers have also just discovered the oldest known supercluster, Hyperion, which formed over 11 billion years ago.

Superclusters are still forming 11 billion years later, but the funny thing about the Universe is that we can see different parts of history all at once.

I JUST HAVE MANY STARS!

El Gordo supercluster

LOOKING BACK

When you peer through a telescope at a distant **star** or **galaxy**, you're actually time traveling. What you get to see from Earth is old news. Light from a distant object may take many, many years to travel through space before it reaches us, so the view you get is a snapshot of how it looked in the distant past.

80 LIGHT YEARS

When a **GIANT** telescope on Earth takes a photo of a galaxy 500 million light years away, we see the galaxy as it looked half a billion years ago.

Amazingly, light can also give us clues about the movement of an object in space. When a galaxy or another object moves toward you, light from it is >squeezed< together, appearing a little more blue when analyzed by scientists and their instruments. This is called **BLUESHIFT**.

When an object is moving away, its light is s t r e t c h e d and appears more red. This is a **REDSHIFT**. A similar thing happens with the sound of sirens on police cars, ambulances, and fire engines. As they approach you, a siren sounds as if it gets higher in pitch only to get lower and lower in pitch the further away it travels.

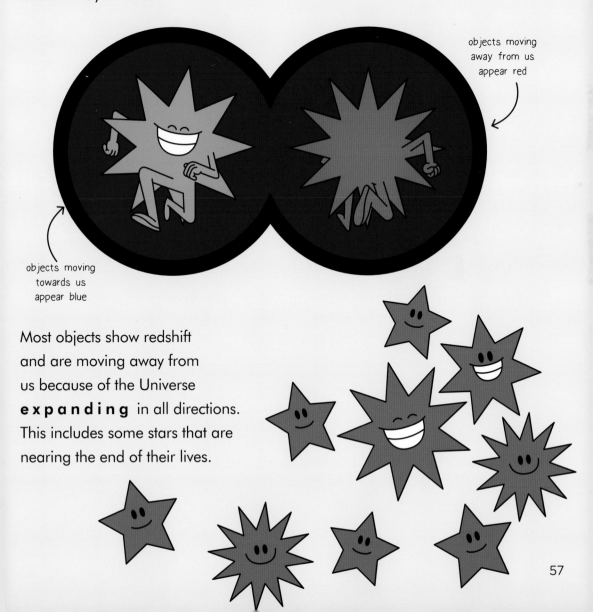

objects moving away from us appear red

objects moving towards us appear blue

Most objects show redshift and are moving away from us because of the Universe **e x p a n d i n g** in all directions. This includes some stars that are nearing the end of their lives.

THE TRAGIC DEATH OF THE STAR

Stars are dying right now. Awful, isn't it? They die in different ways, depending on their **MASS**—the amount of stuff they contain. But it's always for the same reason... they finally run out of fuel to burn.

Cool, tiny stars, less than half of the Sun's mass, have it the best. These **RED DWARFS** use their fuel sparingly and live long, l o n g, l o n g lives, hundreds of billions of years long, before finally dimming to cold, energy-free **BLACK DWARFS**.

Medium-sized stars like our Sun exist for billions of years (but not as long as red dwarfs). When they run out of hydrogen, they swell up to become **RED GIANTS** and eventually use helium as fuel. When their remaining fuel runs out (shame), they puff, puff, puff away their outer layers to become small but brilliant stars called **WHITE DWARFS**.

Those puffed-away outer layers sometimes form eye-catching patterns of rings or shells of gas and dust called planetary nebulae. Some have been given great nicknames, like the **HORSEHEAD** nebula (looks like the head of a horse), the **ANT** nebula (looks like the head and body of an ant), and the **CAT'S EYE** nebula (well, you get the idea).

When it comes to our star, don't fret about the Sun's death. It's not happening anytime soon. Astronomers reckon it has at least 5 billion years of life left, and its death will occur slowly over millions of years.

When it comes to the **BIGGEST** stars, however, their deaths are **MUCH** quicker and more dramatic.

LIVE FAST, DIE YOUNG

GIANT stars might shine brightly, but they don't last (at least, not in star terms). Their lives are measured in millions of years, not billions like our Sun. And if they're 8–40 times more **MASSIVE** than our star, then their ending may be horribly violent and **EXPLOSIVE**.

We call these acts of carnage "**SUPERNOVAE**" and the earliest supernova we've observed—DES16C2nm (catchy name, eh?)—ripped a giant star to shreds about 10.5 billion years ago. Supernovae occurred earlier than that—it's just that we haven't spotted them!

Supernovae can appear brightly in the night sky. One, SN 1006, shone brighter than the nearby planet Venus for three years and was so bright it could be spotted from Earth even during the day.

Here's a four-point guide to impending star apocalypse:

1. A **MASSIVE** star runs out of hydrogen fuel at its core and uses heavier and heavier elements as fuel instead. As it does, it swells up to a **HUGE** size.

2. When the star cannot burn enough fuel to support its **HUGE** size, it suddenly collapses in on itself, pulled toward its core by its own **gravity**.

3. The star will now rebound violently, **BLOWING** its outer layers away with unimaginable violence. The supernova emits as much energy as an entire galaxy of billions of stars. Some of its debris will race away at *speeds* of over 18 million mph.

If the destroyed star was **BIG** enough, its core can sometimes form something mysterious and terrifying...*a black hole*!

61

WHAT'S BLACKER THAN BLACK?

You cannot get **BLACKER** than a *black hole*. Why? Because they give off absolutely no light whatsoever. Not a glimmer. What's more, any light that strays too close to a black hole, gets drawn into it, never to return. Bye!

This means that these strange, **ENORMOUS** astronomical objects are completely invisible—we only know about them because of how we observe light and other objects behaving around the black hole.

WELL, THAT EXPLAINS **A LOT**.

Black holes can form after a **SUPERNOVA**. The devastated star's core collapses beyond belief down to an outrageously dense point with no size at all. It's called a **SINGULARITY**. A second type, **SUPERMASSIVE BLACK HOLES**, lurk at the center of most large galaxies, including the Milky Way. These huge black holes can swallow up even other stars.

Black holes sound kind of scary, but don't worry—they don't go marauding through space, hunting down stars and planets to gobble up. They stay on their orbital paths like stars do.

Both types of black hole exert phenomenal gravity on their neighborhoods. It's not just light. Anything, from a single atom to a giant star, cannot escape a black hole's grip once it strays too close and goes past a point-of-no-return called the **EVENT HORIZON**.

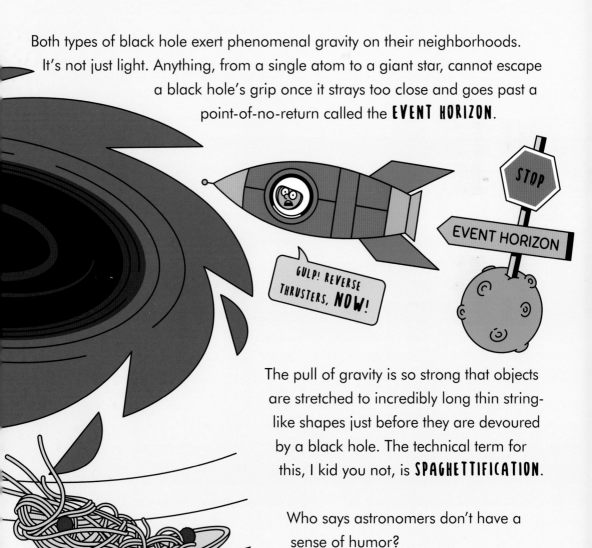

GULP! REVERSE THRUSTERS, **NOW!**

STOP

EVENT HORIZON

The pull of gravity is so strong that objects are stretched to incredibly long thin string-like shapes just before they are devoured by a black hole. The technical term for this, I kid you not, is **SPAGHETTIFICATION**.

Who says astronomers don't have a sense of humor?

PACKING IT ALL IN

Not every supernova creates a black hole. After smaller stars go supernova, they form something called a **neutron star**. If you've ever tried cramming extra clothes into a groaning bag or suitcase, bow down to neutron stars. This is because, at 10–30 km wide, a **neutron star** is no bigger than a city, yet is jam-packed with as much stuff as is found in the Sun.

This makes them very **heavy**. Just a teaspoonful of neutron star would weigh a billion tons on Earth—more than the combined weight of everyone on the planet. If you stood on the surface of a **neutron star**, its powerful gravity would cause you to become part of the neutron star.

I'D OFFER YOU A SPOONFUL OF NEUTRON IN YOUR TEA, BUT I CAN'T LIFT THE SPOON

AND WE ARE ABOUT TO BE CONSUMED BY ITS GRAVITY ANYWAY.

NEUTRON

Some neutron stars send out beams of radio and other waves as they spin, a lot like the beam from a lighthouse. This particular type of neutron star is now called a **PULSAR**, but when first discovered in 1967, they were named Little Green Men (LGM) by British astronomers Jocelyn Bell and Anthony Hewish.

In 1974, Hewish actually won a Nobel Prize for discovering pulsars, but Bell got nothing, nada. Scandalous!

Pretty much everything in the Universe spins, and pulsars are no exception. In fact, they are spinning champions. Most complete a full 360° in a second or less. Other stars would be pulled apart by this dizzying pace, but the iron grip of its super-strong gravity keeps the pulsar together.

TO PUT THIS IN PERSPECTIVE:

- Earth manages one spin every 24 hours.
- A helicopter's blade spins roughly 7 times per second.
- The fastest pulsar spins 716 times per second.

Pretty speedy! But then, a lot of things in space are pretty fast.

FULL SPEED AHEAD

While galaxies developed, the Universe kept on e x p a n d i n g in all directions, but the speed or rate at which it got **BIGGER** slowed down. Scientists think this is due to the gravity of galaxies acting a bit like a brake—a not particularly brilliant one though, as the Universe kept on gr o w i n g.

Then, around 5–6 billion years ago, something remarkable happened. Something stepped on the gas and the expansion of the Universe accelerated. *Whoosh!*

Why's that? Ah. Thought you might ask… er, afraid we simply don't know. Sorry.

Scientists have bundled up many of the mysteries about the expanding Universe into one big bag they've tagged *"dark energy."* The only trouble is no one is quite sure what dark energy is!

DON'T BE ALARMED. This is how some discoveries and theories start out. Scientists may struggle to identify an unknown thing, but can learn about it by observing its effect on other things. It's a bit like studying black holes by their effects on the stars, gas, and other matter they pull in.

Looking to buy up a nice piece of the Universe? Unfortunately, we only know what 3/10ths of it actually is.

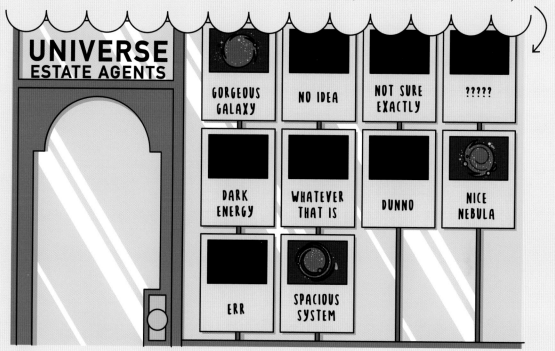

What we do know about *dark energy* is that it makes up a whopping 68% of the entire Universe. Scientists have figured this out through measuring how quickly the Universe is e x p a n d i n g at the moment at certain distances.

A galaxy 35 million light years from us would be moving away at about 467 miles every second. That's like flying from New York to London in one, two, three, four, five, six, seven seconds. Rapid, eh?

HELLO, SOLAR SYSTEM!

It was 4.6 billion years ago, a little after the Universe started accelerating again, in an unremarkable area of space that part of a swirling cloud of gas collapsed in on itself to form a **protostar**. It was surrounded by a large, flattish disc of gas and dust, a bit like a cosmic pizza.

This **protostar** was to prove pretty significant as far as we are concerned, however. It kept on drawing in **MORE** and **MORE** material and heating up until it burst into life about 4.56 billion years ago as the Sun. The Sun drew in and hogged most of the disc's matter, but that still left enough to form other objects.

Dust grains orbiting the new star started clumping together. As they got larger, they collided with others to form larger objects called **PLANETESIMALS** (meaning tiny planets).

Once these gr**ew** to sizes over half a mile or so, their gravity drew in other, smaller pieces of matter, so the planetesimals kept on growing.

PLANETESIMALS clumped together over a period even longer than double math lessons—millions of years. In the part of the disc nearest the blazing hot young Sun, heavier materials with higher boiling points like silicon (a key part of rocks), iron, and other metals survived.

Further out, conditions were far **COOLER** and that's where you'd mostly find lig**hter** materials such as **ICE** and ga**ses** including hydrogen and methane.

PLANET PLANS

Quite how the early solar system looked is anyone's guess! Planetary scientists hotly debate different models of how the system formed. There are also mysteries to think about, such as how **BIG** was the object that knocked the planet Uranus onto its side? And was there once another planet, which was thrown out of the solar system by the gravity of the giant outer planets?

I CAN'T GET UP!

At some point, something knocked Uranus so it spins on its side.

What we do know is that the infant solar system was a pretty violent place with objects crashing into each other all the time. The system quickly developed two distinct zones, an inner, hot zone, and an outer, **COLD ONE**.

SPACE OBJECTS CRASHED INTO EACH OTHER CONSTANTLY DURING THE FORMATION OF OUR SOLAR SYSTEM.

As **PLANETESIMALS** in each zone joined together to make larger and larger objects, two distinct styles of planet would be created. **INNER PLANETS** in the warmer zone (Mercury, Venus, Earth, and Mars) were small, rocky, and had heavy metals in their middle.

The **OUTER PLANETS** (Jupiter, Saturn, Uranus, and Neptune) grew much larger as their gravity attracted huge amounts of gas around them. They ended up as gas or ice giants with no solid outer surface. Both the rocky bodies and gas giants had to pass the planet test.

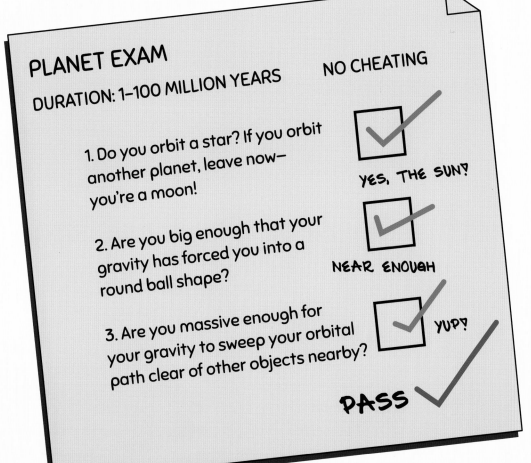

PLANET EXAM

DURATION: 1–100 MILLION YEARS

NO CHEATING

1. Do you orbit a star? If you orbit another planet, leave now— you're a moon!

YES, THE SUN?

2. Are you big enough that your gravity has forced you into a round ball shape?

NEAR ENOUGH

3. Are you massive enough for your gravity to sweep your orbital path clear of other objects nearby?

YUP?

PASS

THE GREAT EIGHT

Until recently, what we know about **PLANETS** comes from studying the eight that make up our solar system. (It used to be nine, but poor old Pluto was relegated by astronomers to a dwarf planet in 2006.)

MERCURY's hot. It's the smallest and closest planet to the Sun.

VENUS' surface is even hotter, about 867 °F—enough to melt lead— thanks to its thick, choking atmosphere.

Life-loving **EARTH** is a real waterworks with 70% of its surface covered in seas and oceans.

MARS is red but dead… as far as we know. Water may have flowed in the past.

JUPITER's a BIG deal. It's twice as massive as all the other planets lumped together.

SATURN is a gas giant, second only to Jupiter, but with the bling of an elaborate ring system.

URANUS is cold, icy, and orbits the Sun tilted on its side.

NEPTUNE is similar in size to Uranus but even farther from the Sun.

The word "**PLANET**" comes from the Greek for "wanderer" as planets appeared to wander across the **night sky**. The planets' orbits vary greatly—Mercury's takes just 88 days, while Neptune's lasts 165 years.

Early in their lives, some planets shifted their orbits dramatically. Neptune and Uranus took a big hike farther away from the Sun, while Jupiter moved in then out (but as far as we know, didn't shake it all about). At its closest, Jupiter was only 1½ times farther away from the Sun than Earth. Now, it's more than 5 times farther away.

WE'RE OFF!

MOONING AROUND

MOONS are the must-have fashion accessory for planets (and some asteroids as well). These mostly rocky objects orbit a planet just like the planet orbits a star, kept in place by **gravity**.

Earth's Moon was the only moon we knew about until Italian scientist **GALILEO GALILEI** pointed his brand new telescope toward Jupiter just over 400 years ago and spotted four new ones. Since then, more than 200 further moons have been discovered, the latest in late 2019 whistling around Saturn.

While Venus has no moons and Earth just one (the Moon), some planets really overdo it. That we are aware of, Neptune has 14, Uranus 27, Saturn 82, and Jupiter 79 moons. The largest solar system moons, **GANYMEDE** and **TITAN**, are bigger than the planet Mercury.

Moons form in different ways. Many were created around the same time as their parent planet and were drawn into orbit as the planet formed. Others, like our Moon, are the result of a large object striking the planet. Around 4.5 billion years ago, the newly formed Earth was struck by an object the size of Mars. Ouch! The impact threw up debris into space, which clumped together quickly to form the Moon.

Our Moon is covered in **CRATERS** and is lifeless, except when 12 American astronauts in six Apollo Lunar Modules landed on it between 1969 and 1972. One astronaut even hit golf shots on its surface. Fore!

MORE ON MOONS

Moons are slaves to **gravity**, which keeps them in orbit... mostly. Some moons are creeping slowly a w a y from their planet—in the case of our Moon, it is a measly 1.5 in. a year.

Most moons, including our Moon, are also **TIDALLY LOCKED**. Gravity between a moon and its planet means the moon spins round at the same rate that they orbit their planet. The result? The same side of the moon always faces its planet.

The same side of a moon will always face its planet, so who knows what goes on on the far side?

Our solar system boasts some seriously cool moons, including:

ENCELADUS → This shiny, bright white moon of Saturn shoots ice, water, and dust out of ice geysers on its surface.

MIRANDA → The surface of this moon of Uranus is scarred with canyons, 12 times deeper than the Grand Canyon on Earth.

IO → There's more volcano action on this moon of Jupiter than anywhere else in the solar system. As a result, Io's surface gets constant facelifts as fresh lava flows.

TITAN → Boasts a thicker atmosphere than Earth, with orange clouds as well as lakes and seas full of liquid methane on its surface.

EUROPA → Covered in ice, this moon of Jupiter is thought to harbor oceans of water beneath—an incredibly exciting thought for space scientists.

DEIMOS AND PHOBOS
Mars' two small, potato-shaped moons are thought to be victims of kidnapping, captured by the planet's gravity. They were originally wandering chunks of rock called asteroids.

ASTEROIDS

Visit a building site and you're bound to see leftover rubble. **ASTEROIDS** are solar system rubble left over from its formation 4.6 billion years ago. Most are **ROCKY**, although some contain **METAL** or are all iron and nickel.

LET'S ROCK!

I PREFER METAL!

ASTEROIDS all orbit the Sun. They vary from 3 ft-wide super-pebbles up to 591 mile-wide **CERES**. Most asteroids hang out in a b r o a d belt orbiting the Sun between Mars and Jupiter.

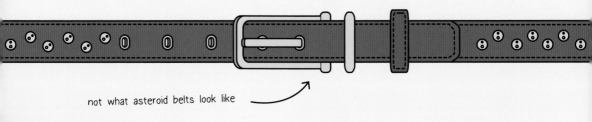

not what asteroid belts look like

WHO YOU CALLING A BULLY?

More than 1.1 million asteroids, each measuring half a mile or more, are found in the **ASTEROID BELT**. They may have nearly formed another planet in the distant past, but were bullied by Jupiter and its epic gravity, which stopped them clumping together. Over a million asteroids sounds like a huge amount, but astronomers have done the math and reckon, all added together, they would barely equal one-tenth of the mass of the Moon.

ASTEROIDS sometimes collide with each other and **SLAM** into other objects including Earth, especially in the past. Impacts now are very rare. Good job, too, as large ones can be catastrophic. Earth suffered a hefty asteroid impact around 65.5 million years ago. It landed in what is now southern Mexico and threw up so much dust into the atmosphere, it caused major climate change. This led to 75% of all animals, including mighty **DINOSAURS**, dying out. Yikes!

METEORS, in comparison, are usually far less scary.

METEOR-WHAT?

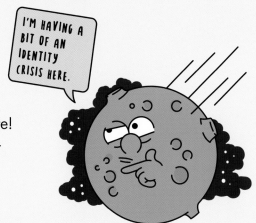

When is a meteor not a meteor? When it is a meteoroid or a meteorite! Yes, the same piece of space rock or metal can be all three things. It all depends on precisely where it is.

METEOROIDS are often quite small and left over from the formation of our solar system. Sometimes, they form when a collision chips away a piece of asteroid.

These meteoroids and their millimeter-small cousins, micrometeoroids, travel around in space, usually not bothering anyone or anything. But if a meteoroid enters Earth's atmosphere and burns up, it gets a name change. It's now called a **METEOR** (or a shooting star).

Large numbers of meteors reaching Earth at the same time are called a **METEOR SHOWER**. They can form spectacular displays across the night sky. Some, like the Perseids and Leonids, occur regularly every year. A tiny fraction of these meteors don't totally burn up. They muscle their way through Earth's atmosphere to land on the planet's surface. Time for a new name to greet their arrival… **METEORITES**.

NOT WHAT A METEOR SHOWER IS LIKE.

OH WELL, THERE WASN'T MUCH ON ANYWAY.

An estimated 500 meteorites land on Earth each year. But don't worry. Most fall into water or land in remote areas. Only one person for definite has been injured directly by a falling meteorite— an American lady called **ANN ELIZABETH HODGES** in 1954. She was minding her own business at home when a 9 lb meteorite crashed through the roof of her home, leaving a few bruises!

Some meteorites are recovered for scientists to study. The biggest ever, the **HOBA** meteorite, landed 80,000 years ago in Namibia in Africa but was only found in 1920. It still lies where it landed and is now a visitor attraction.

HAIRY STARS

Another type of astronomical object is the **COMET**. The ancient Greeks called them "**HAIRY STARS**" while we nickname them cosmic or dirty snowballs.

The word comet comes from the Greek kometes, meaning 'hairy star'.

When the solar system was forming, the edge of the disc farthest from the Sun was freezing **COLD**. Dust grains there became coated with ice and frozen gases a little like yogurt-coated raisins... Mmmm. Over time, the grains clumped together to form millions of comet nuclei, each a few miles wide.

COMETS orbit the Sun, mostly from huge distances away. Some comets' orbits, though, bring them much closer to us and the Sun, and that's when the fun starts. Going past Jupiter, comets really start to feel the burn from the Sun's energy. Parts of the comet nucleus turn into gas. They form a glowing cloud around the comet nucleus called a **COMA**. More gas and dust from the comet form long **TAILS**, stretching millions of miles behind.

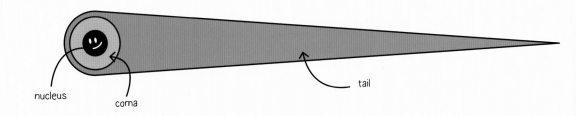

nucleus

coma

tail

Comets' orbits vary **H U G E L Y.** Some just cannot stay away. These short-period comets orbit the Sun every few years or decades. Others only offer a once-in-a-lifetime chance to see. Comet **HYAKUTAKE**, for instance, blazed a spectacular trail through the night sky in 1996. If you weren't around to see it... tough! Its orbit is so big, it won't be back for 70,000 years.

Comets may be a relatively rare and wondrous sight today, but in Earth's early years, scientists believe they rained down on our planet's surface, just one of a wave of objects that bombarded early Earth.

EARLY EARTH

Between its formation and about 3.8 billion years ago, large numbers of **ASTEROIDS** and **COMETS** struck and battered early Earth's surface. But it wasn't only the comet storms that made it very different from the fab and groovy place you live on and enjoy today. For hundreds of millions of years, our planet was more unpleasant than a busload of bullies.

At time, Earth was unbearably hot, with its surface covered in red-hot melting rock and cracks, oozing lava. Vast numbers of **VOLCANOES** erupted, releasing more lava and poisonous, stinky gases such as methane, carbon dioxide, and ammonia.

Early Earth's extreme heat saw metals, especially iron and nickel, melt out of rocks. As they were **denser** and **heavier** than the surrounding rock, they sank to the planet's middle. There, they formed a hot core of two parts—a SOLID INNER CORE and a LIQUID OUTER CORE. A thick layer of rock, called MANTLE, built up around the core. It's now about 1,800 miles thick. Heat from the core keeps the mantle slightly soft and bendy.

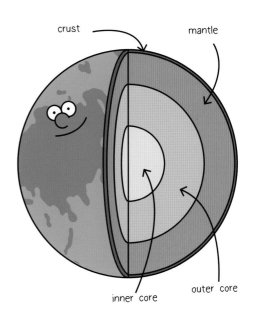

crust

mantle

outer core

inner core

Earth's outer layer cooled to form a thin, rocky CRUST, giving the planet a diameter of 7,926 miles through the EQUATOR—the imaginary line that runs around the centre of the planet. A rocky crust sounds tough and solid, but as it sort of floats on top of the bendy mantle, big chunks of the crust are sometimes on the move.

85

BREAKING UP IS HARD TO DO

It's hard to imagine, but Earth has managed at least three big break-ups in its past. Whole **LANDMASSES** have moved together and drifted a p a r t a number of times during its history.

It's all down to how Earth's crust formed a number of **GIGANTIC** slabs, we think 2–3 billion years ago. These slabs (or **TECTONIC PLATES** if you want to get all science-y and technical) sit on top of the Earth's mantle. They fit together a little like panels of a soccer ball but can move a couple of inches each year.

A couple of inches sounds puny, but over time, it all + adds + up.

The last major break-up began around 200 million years ago. At the time, all of Earth's land formed one giant lump or supercontinent called **PANGAEA**. Movement of the plates split Pangaea up, firstly into two massive chunks called **GONDWANALAND** and **LAURASIA**.

These two landmasses broke up into smaller pieces, eventually forming the continents we know today.

The boundaries between **TECTONIC PLATES** are often pretty active places. The grinding together of plates, for example, can cause **EARTHQUAKES** and **VOLCANIC ERUPTIONS**. And when tectonic plates collide head-on, they can sometimes form mountain ranges. India was once an island, but drifted northward and 40–50 million years ago thumped into the Eurasia plate. **CRUNCH!** As the two landmasses collided, they drove rock up to form the mighty Himalayas—the world's highest mountain range.

LIFE'S A GAS!

Like a terrible party with no music, snacks, or interesting guests, in the beginning, early Earth lacked a decent **ATMOSPHERE**. There had been some hydrogen and helium surrounding the planet, but these light gases didn't stick around for long, before drifting up and away into space.

However, all that **VOLCANIC ACTIVITY** caused by the Earth's plates shifting and grinding released lots of gases from inside the planet. This is called outgassing and included carbon dioxide, ammonia, and hot water vapor.

These **heavier** gases stuck around, held in place by gravity. Much of the water vapor cooled, turned into liquid, and fell as rain, helping to fill the planet's early oceans. That's when things really began to get interesting.

Sometime around 4 billion years ago, no one knows quite how, life began on Earth. **TA-DA!**

One theory is that a "**SOUP**" of the right sort of chemicals developed and molecules started reproducing themselves. Among Earth's earliest inhabitants were **SINGLE-CELLED MICROORGANISMS** and **BACTERIA**. These early organisms got their energy from various different chemical reactions. But around 2.5 billion years ago, certain types of bacteria and algae developed the ability to **PHOTOSYNTHESIZE**.

PRIMORDIAL LIFE SOUP

PHOTOSYNTHESIS is the process whereby plants and algae create food for themselves using carbon dioxide, water, and energy from sunlight.

This new development was a Very Big Deal… Why? Because photosynthesis also creates oxygen. You know, that stuff that you (and other lifeforms) love to breathe? Photosynthesis set the stage for more life to **EVOLVE**.

LET'S BREATHE SOME **LIFE** INTO THIS PARTY!

GET MORE LIFE

Over time, all this **PHOTOSYNTHESIS** created the lovely oxygen-rich atmosphere that we enjoy today. As well as being great for breathing, the atmosphere shields Earth's surface from harmful rays from the Sun, keeps the planet warm, and circulates winds and weather. **TOP JOB.**

Combined with a good amount of **WATER**, and a location just the right distance from the Sun to be not too hot or too cold, the conditions on Earth were just right for life to really flourish.

GREAT LOCATION
PERFECT DISTANCE FROM THE SUN FOR MILD CLIMATE.
RUNNING WATER
LOTS OF IT
INSULATION?
YUP – AN ATMOSPHERE. IT'S THE PERFECT HOME!

More **COMPLEX LIFEFORMS** emerged around 560 million years ago, although they were still very different from animals we would recognize today, mostly being simple tube- or fern-shaped creatures. For a long time, living things stayed in the ocean. Then, around 500 million years ago, critters started crawling out of the seas and onto land.

Among the first living things to brave the dry outdoors were early **INSECTS** and ancestors of **CRABS** and **SPIDERS**, followed by freaky **FISH** with fins adapted into little legs.

PLANTS spread over land not that long after. The first trees and forests appeared about 380 million years ago. **MAMMALS** and **DINOSAURS** both arrived 220–240 million years ago. Some dinosaurs later evolved into birds. For 160 million years, dinosaurs ruled the Earth. During their reign, flowers first appeared.

Dinosaurs and three-quarters of all species died out around 65 million years ago. Curse you, giant asteroid impact! But life continued, and mammals and insects came to dominate the planet. Life continued to spawn a great variety of new species including… you, yes, YOU!

HEY PEOPLE, YOU'RE LATE!

Eventually, some of those mammals evolved into human beings or "HOMO SAPIENS," somewhere around 300,000 to 200,000 years ago. Compared to the entire history of the Universe, we have been around for just a blink of an eye.

If the entire 13.7 billion year history of the Universe is SQUEEZED into a single year, with the Big Bang at the start of JANUARY 1ST, then:

JANUARY 1

BETTER GET MYSELF TOGETHER!

The Milky Way began coming together in MARCH.

OH MARCH ALREADY.

MARCH 1

DECEMBER 17

The solar system and Earth formed at the start of September, while the first fish arrived around the 17TH OF DECEMBER but...

Dinosaurs didn't debut until **CHRISTMAS DAY**...

I HOPE IT'S THAT TRICERATOPS I WANTED.

DECEMBER
25

SORRY I'M LATE.

TROUBLE PARKING THE CHARIOT.

DECEMBER
31

People as we know them (*Homo sapiens*) didn't turn up until after **11PM** on **NEW YEAR'S EVE**.

All of recorded human history happened in the last minutes of the **LAST DAY** of the year. The ancient Romans, for example, didn't arrive until five seconds before midnight.

This Universe-in-a-year caper is known as the **COSMIC CALENDAR**. It was made popular by astronomy legend **CARL SAGAN** and highlights just how little time you, I, and the rest of the human race have been around.

So things have been pretty busy on our little old planet recently. But there are a lot of other planets out there, and not just the other seven in our solar system...

PLANETS EVERYWHERE

In 1992, astronomers captured the first cast-iron proof that planets outside the solar system do exist. Since then, over 4,057 of these **EXOPLANETS** have been found, orbiting stars other than the Sun… with thousands more likely to be confirmed soon.

Astronomers have to be really canny when they go exoplanet hunting, as distant planets are far harder to spot in the night sky than bright stars. Most are found as they **TRANSIT**—travel in front of their parent star and block a little of the star's light.

> AMAZING! I'VE DISCOVERED A NEW STAR, AND A NEW EXOPLANET!

EXOPLANETS can be a wild bunch…

Some are bigger than **JUPITER**, but red hot enough to melt steel and other metals. The surface of the Kepler-70b exoplanet for example, is a thermometer-busting 12,632 °F—hotter than the surface of the Sun. Other exoplanets are seriously *fast movers*, whizzing around their star in hours, not 365¼ days like we do. 55 Cancri e is the hard man of exoplanets—it may be made of solid diamond.

some speedy exoplanets completely orbit their suns within hours

HD 189733b is thought to rain molten glass onto its surface.

Beta Pictoris b is surrounded by clouds of deadly carbon monoxide. None of these sound like great places for your summer holiday.

What planet hunters are really looking for are less **EXTREME EXOPLANETS**, which lie just the right distance away from their star so that they're not too hot and not too cold. This region in space is called the **GOLDILOCKS ZONE** after the infamous porridge thief.

A planet in this zone has a greater chance of liquid water existing on its surface, and—if it also has a rich atmosphere—there's the tiny, tantalizing possibility of **ALIEN LIFE**! Woo hoo!

ARE WE ALONE?

Our planet is pretty crowded. We've got over 7.7 billion people and gazillions of other living things on our planet to keep us company—from microscopic bacteria to 100 ft-long blue whales. But what about other planets?

I mean, is Earth alone? Is it really the only place in the **WHOLE UNIVERSE** to harbor life? Some scientists think it's pretty unlikely.

After all, there are billions of galaxies, each with billions of stars, many of which have planets orbiting them. Among these **TRILLIONS** of planets, surely the chances of one or more containing water and everything else life requires is **HIGH**.

The real trouble seems to be finding them! The **V A S T** distances in space mean we struggle to explore it. So far, we've barely stepped out past our own front door.

Our most distant spacecraft, **VOYAGER I** and **II**, were launched in 1977 and are only now leaving the solar system. They won't get close to other planets for at least 40,000 years, possibly longer.

On board each Voyager is a gold record containing sounds and pictures of Earth, just in case aliens encounter it and have invented record players…

RADIO WAVES travel far faster (speed of light *fast*) and farther than spacecraft. So, scientists beam out signals and scour the skies, using giant radio telescopes, to seek out signals from space that may be from intelligent life elsewhere.

And if it existed, extraterrestrial life might appear quite different from lifeforms we're used to. Would we even recognize an alien if we encountered one?

AND WOULD THEY RECOGNIZE US?

THE END OF THE WORLD

So we've talked about how it all began. What about how it will end? Well, the good news is the end of the world won't happen for a *l o n g* while, so relax, do your homework, recycling, and other efforts to keep the planet clean and healthy.

IF YOU DON'T WANT TO KNOW THE ENDING, LOOK AWAY NOW...

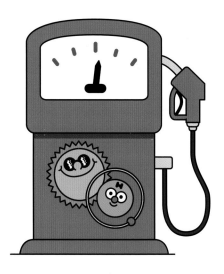

If you're still reading on bravely, good for you and let me start with some good news. Our Sun is roughly halfway through its time as a star on the main sequence. Scientists reckon that it has enough hydrogen fuel in the tank to shine brighter and brighter for at least five billion more years. Yay!

But long before its hydrogen fuel runs out, the Sun's increasing brightness will probably have fried most species off the planet. **NOT SO YAY, EH?**

You see, the Sun is gradually increasing the amount of energy it sends out into space. **NASA** estimates around a 10% increase every one billion years. Big increases could disrupt Earth's atmosphere, evaporate all its oceans, rivers, and other liquid water away, and cause life on the planet to cease to exist.
I'm afraid it gets worse.

When its hydrogen does run out, the Sun, as a medium mass star, will swell up to become a **RED GIANT**. This bloated star will grOW and grOW until it engulfs Mercury and Venus as it expands to over 2,000 times its current size. As it balloons, Earth may also be engulfed by the Sun's outer layers in a very **FIERY FINALE**.

HOW WILL THE UNIVERSE END?

The end of our planet doesn't mean the end of the Universe though. So how will the **WHOLE UNIVERSE** end? Well, the truth is (whisper it quietly, especially in front of big-brained space scientists)… we're not sure. Shhhhhh.

JUST DON'T ASK ME HOW THE UNIVERSE WILL END…

PLEASE!

What the same big-brained space scientists *do* know, however, is that the universe isn't going to end for millions, probably billions and billions, of years. In short, you're free to plan that cinema trip next Tuesday as well as your next holiday.

There are a number of **THEORIES** for how the Universe might end. Some are highly unlikely…

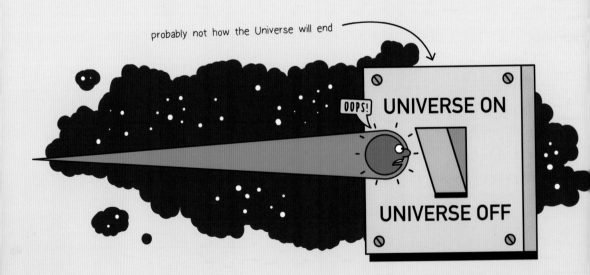

probably not how the Universe will end

OOPS! UNIVERSE ON

UNIVERSE OFF

Others are thought to be more plausible. Of these, first up is the **BIG FREEZE**. Brrrr!

The opposite of Earth's fiery ending, this sees the Universe e x p a n d i n g and cooling for billions, possibly trillions, of years.

Eventually, stars would fizzle out and fade, never to be replaced, the lights will go out, and **HEAT DEATH** occurs. This is where everything throughout space is the same temperature— around or just above absolute zero, which is a desperately **CHILLY** −459.67 °F.

No heat energy means **NOTHING** interesting will happen again... probably ever. Like being trapped in your most deadly dull relative's house... **FOREVER**.

Too dreary for words and not dramatic enough for you? Well, perhaps we might get a more exciting finale, something like the Universe getting **RIPPED** or **CRUNCHED**...

RIPPED OR CRUNCHED?

Which ending would you prefer? Neither of these big finishes sound particularly pleasant, I'm afraid. Both theories depend on which one of two **POWERFUL FORCES** come out on top in the ultimate wrestling match.

You see, the Universe is engaged in a constant struggle between these two epic forces.

In the blue corner, the force of **EXPANSION** as the Universe increases in size in every direction.

In the red corner, the force of **GRAVITY**, keen on keeping it all together.

BIG RIP

In an ending known as the **BIG RIP**, expansion wins. The Universe expands faster and faster. Galaxies, then stars, then individual atoms, and finally parts of atoms would move farther away from each other, tearing everything apart. Nasty!

BIG CRUNCH

If **GRAVITY** wins out, the end may be quite different. Like a cosmic bungee cord, gravity would put a stop to the Universe's expansion, and would draw galaxies closer and closer together. Eventually, they would all collide [**CRASH!**] and merge, bumping temperatures up into millions of degrees.

CHAOS!

The entire Universe would collapse in on itself and shrink to a single, mind-numbingly small, dense, and hot point. Sound familiar…? It should, as we're back to where it all started, and the **BIG BANG**!

HOW WE KNOW WHAT WE KNOW

Whew! That was quite a wild ride, wasn't it? Given how mind-melting it all is, it's a reasonable question to ask how we know any of this stuff. Well, a lot of very bright people (and a few dim ones) have devoted their lives to studying space.

People began charting objects moving across the **night sky** thousands of years ago. Some based stories, myths, and even religions on these objects. Others got practical, using the night sky to measure the passing of time to create calendars or to find their way at night by following certain **stars**.

Some particularly patient souls built up real spotters' guides of **stars**. Top star catalogers included ancient Greeks such as **HIPPARCHUS** and **PTOLEMY** as well as the great **DANE, TYCHO BRAHE**, who lost most of his nose in a duel and wore a false one made of brass and wax. All these brilliant astronomers studied stars just with their eyes.

The arrival of **TELESCOPES** in the 1600s changed everything. Optical telescopes use lenses or mirrors to gather in, bend, and focus light from space to help magnify distant objects.

Using telescopes and other scientific instruments, people have discovered millions of mind-blowing objects and phenomena in space, from exploding stars to the Universe's ultimate vacuum cleaners, *black holes*.

In the 20th century, **ROCKET POWER** launched machines into space for the first time. Robotic probes whizzed past or landed on **PLANETS, MOONS,** and **COMETS**, sending back pictures and other scientific data. All this exciting new information helped lead to new theories about how the Universe works. But there's so much more to discover and we may have only scratched the surface, because the Universe is unbelievably **HUGE!** How huge? Let's see.

In recent decades, NASA has sent four Rover robots to Mars to send back scientific information and photos of the planet's surface.

SIZING IT UP

People have always liked to do their exploring up close and personal on Earth. Exploring the Universe in the same way is mostly impossible because everything is simply too f a r away.

The farthest anyone has traveled from Earth is **248,654 MILES** (well done, the three astronauts in Apollo 13). Sounds impressive, but it's just a gnat's kneecap in space. For example, Apollo 13 would have needed to travel 372 times farther than it did just to reach the Sun.

The Universe is so outrageously **VAST**, simple kilometers and miles don't cut it. Scientists need a far bigger tape measure to describe distances. So they use the distance light travels in a year as a measure.

LIGHT is a seriously fast mover, racing along at 186,282 miles every second. Forget Ferraris*, in the time it takes you to read this sentence (3–4 seconds) light has traveled over half a million miles. That's 25 round-the-world trips. **Whoosh!**

Light travels **5.87 TRILLION MILES** in a year. A trillion is a million million, or if you prefer it in a number—1,000,000,000,000. That makes a light year 63,240 times the average distance between Earth and the Sun. Wow! I should have warned you there were some big numbers coming. Sorry!

Now, no one knows the precise size of the whole Universe, because we cannot see the edge—if there is one. All we do know is that the observable Universe is at least 93 thousand million light years across!

This **PHENOMENAL SIZE** makes it all the more astounding that the Universe started out smaller than the smallest thing you can possibly imagine.

SPACE EXPLORATION TIMELINE

It took a lot of hard work, ingenuity, luck, and money to get people and machines into space to explore. So far, fewer than 600 men and women have become astronauts, but the future may see **SPACE TOURISM** with hundreds and thousands more following.

~800S CE

The Chinese discover gunpowder (made by mixing a substance called saltpeter with charcoal and sulfur) is explosive when lit by a flame.

~1200S CE

The first rockets are made in China, fueled by gunpowder packed into bamboo tubes and used as a weapon of shock and awe against enemy forces.

1924

Rocket-mad twelve-year-old boy Wernher von Braun lets a toy car race through the streets of the German city of Berlin powered by rockets. Von Braun will later become NASA's leading rocket scientist.

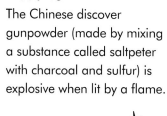

1923

German scientist Hermann Oberth publishes a book that explains how powerful rockets could escape Earth's gravity and head into space. Hermann's handbook inspires many other rocketeers.

1926

American Robert H. Goddard flies the first rocket using liquid fuel. It only travels 40 ft high and lands in a nearby cabbage patch… but it's a start! Goddard will go on to build higher-flying test rockets.

1929

American astronomer Edwin Hubble provides evidence that the Universe is expanding. It is BIG news. So are Georges Lemaître's ideas (1927–31) that later become known as the Big Bang Theory.

1500S

According to legend, one Chinese official, Wan Hu, fitted a chair with 47 rockets in an attempt to reach the Moon... it didn't end well for him. Think blazing fireball... Oh dear.

1687

Genius scientist Isaac Newton explains the force of gravity and the scientific laws of how things move in his groundbreaking book, *Principia Mathematica*. Newton's laws of motion explain how rockets, spacecraft, planets, and moons all travel through space.

STOP DAYDREAMING IN CLASS!

1903

Russian schoolteacher Konstantin Tsiolkovsky suggests how rockets could be used to explore space.

1932

Karl Jansky detects the first radio waves coming from space, starting the valuable field of radio astronomy. Nice one, Karl!

1942

The German V-2 rocket-powered missile, which can reach altitudes of 55–125 miles, is first launched.

1947

Fruit flies become the first earthlings in space as they are launched to an altitude of 68 miles above Earth in an American-launched V2 rocket.

1962

Mariner 2 becomes the first machine sent from Earth to reach another planet, traveling relatively close to Venus and measuring the planet for the first time.

1963

The "Cosmic Microwave Background" is discovered by Arno Penzias and Robert Wilson using a radio telescope.

1966

The Soviet Union's Luna 9 probe becomes the first machine to make a successful soft landing on (rather than crashing into) the Moon.

1957

The Soviet Union launches the first artificial satellite, called Sputnik, using an R-7 rocket missile. It orbits Earth for almost three months and becomes world news. The Soviet's rivals, the USA, are spooked and vowed to send up their own satellite…

…which they manage the following year with the launch of Explorer I. Guess who designed the rocket that launched it? Wernher Von Braun.

1961

Yuri Gagarin from the Soviet Union becomes the first person in space inside the tiny, cramped Vostok 1 spacecraft. Two years later, Valentina Tereshkova, who had trained with Gagarin, becomes the first woman in space.

1969

The Apollo 11 Lunar Module carries the first astronauts to land on the Moon—Neil Armstrong and Edwin "Buzz" Aldrin. The pair spend some hours on the lunar surface planting a flag, setting up experiments and collecting 49.7 lbs of moon rocks and soil to take back home. Epic!

1972

The Pioneer 10 space probe becomes the first human-made machine to fly-by the giant planet, Jupiter.

1975

Venera 9 sends the first-ever photo of another planet's surface after landing on Venus. Its predecessor, Venera 7, managed to land five years earlier but was not fitted with a camera. Doh! Venera 9 only lasts an hour before the hostile conditions stop it working.

AAGH, I'M MELTING...

WOO HOO!

1984

Astronaut Bruce McCandless makes the first spacewalk without being tied to his spacecraft by a tether. Instead, Bruce whizzed around in an amazing jetpack-type arrangement called the Manned Maneuvering Unit (MMU).

1982

Svetlana Savitskaya becomes only the second female astronaut, 19 years after the first. It's a scandal when you think about it.

1990

The Hubble Space Telescope is launched. Lots of back-slapping occurred back on Earth until it was discovered it needed glasses! The Hubble's lens had a small flaw, which had to be corrected by fitting a sort of high-tech contact lens called COSTAR in 1993. From that point on, the Hubble was on top form and would take hundreds of thousands of images.

CAN YOU READ THE THIRD-FROM-BOTTOM LINE FOR ME?

1976

Viking 1 and Viking 2 both land successfully on Mars. These lander probes send back the first photos and analysis of soil from the Red Planet's surface.

1977

Voyager 1 and 2 are launched to explore the outer solar system. Both probes are still going strong! By November 2019, Voyager 1 was around 14 billion miles away from Earth, while Voyager 2 was the first probe to fly past Uranus (1986) and Neptune (1989).

1981

NASA's Space Shuttle—the first reusable spacecraft—makes its debut. A fleet of Space Shuttles make over 130 missions into space, taking off vertically like a rocket but gliding back to Earth like an aircraft.

ARE YOU SURE ABOUT THIS PATIO AND OUTDOOR POOL?

1990s

The Hubble takes a series of truly stunning and scientifically important images including the Deep Field image which showed over 3,000 distant galaxies.

1998

The first part of the International Space Station (ISS) is launched. Over the 15 years that followed, more and more modules and parts would be added to make the biggest ever home for astronauts in space.

I HEARD SOMEONE SAY THERE WAS A POOL?

2001

Dennis Tito becomes the world's first space tourist, spending almost eight days in space on board a Soyuz spacecraft and the ISS. Mr. Tito paid a cool $20 million for the privilege!

2003

China becomes the third nation, after the USA and the Soviet Union, to send an astronaut into space. The lucky man is Yang Liwei, aboard the Shenzhou 5 spacecraft.

2015

The New Horizons probe reaches Pluto nine years after it was launched from Earth.

2010

Dust samples from the asteroid Itokawa, gathered by the groovy Japanese Hayabusa space probe in 2005, finally make it back to Earth for scientists to analyse.

2016

The world's largest radio telescope, called FAST and measuring a whopping 1,640 ft wide, begins observations in China.

2017

After her third mission on board the ISS, American astronaut Peggy Whitson holds the record for the most time spent by a woman in space, 665 days.

I CAN'T EVEN REMEMBER WHAT GRAVITY FEELS LIKE!

OH, THE SHAME!

2006

Poor old Pluto is downgraded in status from a planet to a dwarf planet.

2008

While performing a spacewalk at the ISS, astronaut Heidemarie Stefanyshyn-Piper loses grip of a toolbag, which drifts off into space. That's a pretty expensive lost property incident, as the bag and the tools inside were worth around $100,000!

2009

The Kepler spacecraft is launched on a mega mission to map stars and find new planets outside the solar system. It's a hit, as it goes on to discover over 2,660 exoplanets.

2020

The ISS celebrates 20 years of continually being inhabited by astronauts—over 240 of them. During this time, thousands of space experiments have been performed.

I WAS ONLY AFTER A TELESCOPE FOR MY 9 YEAR OLD DAUGHTER

BUT THIS IS THE BEST AROUND!

2021

The expected launch year of the James Webb Space Telescope (JWST). Designed to be much more powerful than the Hubble, the JWST—along with the ground-based ELT (Extremely Large Telescope), which will be completed four years later—may revolutionize what we know about the Universe. Can't wait!

SPACE PLACES

While a trip to the Moon or Mars is not yet available (shame), there are some great locations here on Earth where you can learn more about the wonders of the Universe.

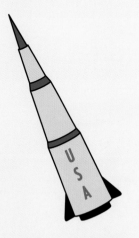

KENNEDY SPACE CENTER, USA
https://www.kennedyspacecenter.com/
Space nerds cannot miss the launch site of NASA's Apollo missions to the Moon, which is packed with historic spacecrafts, rockets, and exhibits for you to enjoy as part of a trip to Florida. You may even get to tour around with or hear a talk by a veteran NASA astronaut.

STAR CITY, RUSSIA
http://www.gctc.su/
This super-cool site in Moscow is where Russian cosmonauts have been trained since the 1960s. In the past, the Yuri Gagarin Cosmonaut Training Centre (to give it its full name) was highly secret, but now you can do tours and experience what it's like to be a cosmonaut, including eating space food, wearing a space suit, and operating a spaceship.

LE BOURGET AIR AND SPACE MUSEUM, FRANCE
https://www.museeairespace.fr/en/
Found near Paris, this museum contains giant Ariane rockets, a large stargazing arena, and the Planète Pilote zone where visitors can mimic astronaut training and learn more about living on board a space station.

GDC OBSERVATORY, AUSTRALIA

https://gravitycentre.com.au/observatory/

Situated in pristine Western Australian bushland, with dark skies, this awesome observatory offers visitors the opportunity to stargaze under the guidance of expert astronomers. They also run fantastic Aboriginal Astronomy sessions with Indigenous elders who share expert knowledge and stories about the night sky.

NATIONAL SPACE CENTRE, UK

https://spacecentre.co.uk/

From its giant rocket tower and full-size mock-up of International Space Station modules to an interactive Moon base and giant star dome, this visitor attraction in Leicester is a must for all space hounds.

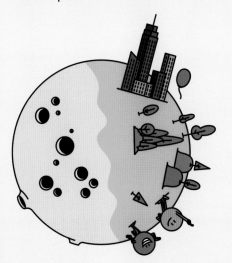

GLASGOW SCIENCE CENTRE, UK

https://www.glasgowsciencecentre.org

Enjoy this visitor attraction's space zone, with exhibits on stars and galaxies, and how space exploration has revolutionized our knowledge, and watch amazing movies and presentations in the center's planetarium.

TO INFINITY... AND BEYOND!

Want to know more? Of course you do! These sites, videos, and books will help you take your own personal voyage further.

BOOKS AND MAGS

Astrophysics for Young People in a Hurry – Neil deGrasse Tyson (W. W. Norton & Co., 2019)
Written by one of America's most celebrated astronomers and physicists, this book delves into the creation of the Universe.

Ask the Astronaut – Tom Jones (Smithsonian Books, 2015)
A bumper book of answers to puzzling questions about the Universe and spaceflight, from a veteran NASA astronaut.

The Astronomy Book: Big Ideas Simply Explained (DK, 2017)
Lots of text on the breakthroughs and milestones in the history of studying and understanding the Universe.

Star Talk – Neil deGrasse Tyson, Jeffrey Simons, Charles Liu (National Geographic, 2019)
Another blockbusting questions-and-answers book about space travel, the solar system, and the Universe.

Cosmos: The Infographic Book of Space – Stuart Lowe & Chris North (Aurum Press, 2017)
A cool and funky visual look at astronomy and the Universe.

The Race To Space – Clive Gifford (words & pictures, 2019)
Learn about the fascinating and surprising competition
between nations to escape Earth's gravity and explore space.

WEBSITES

http://astronoteen.org/
If you are or are nearly a teen and are interested in astronomy, then this website, started by a 14-year-old astronomy nut a few years back, is definitely for you. It's full of features to spot in the night sky.

https://www.zooniverse.org/projects/zookeeper/galaxy-zoo
A project in which volunteers help identify, describe, and classify galaxies spotted by the Dark Energy Camera Legacy Survey (DECaLS). Anyone can do it!

https://imagine.gsfc.nasa.gov/
NASA's webpages for teenagers interested in space are a treasure trove of news and features including a useful series of answers to the BIG questions.

https://www.rocketstem.org/
Online space and spaceflight magazine aimed at the next generation of rocket scientists and astronomers.

https://www.spacetelescope.org/images/archive/top100/
One hundred of the Hubble Space Telescope's greatest images of the Universe. Prepare to be stunned.

COSMIC QUIZ

Now you know have read the entire history of the Universe, will you be able to answer these out-of-this-world questions?

1   What was the name given to the first teeny-weeny tiny fraction of a second at the very beginning of the Universe's existence?

2   What is the most abundant element in the Universe?

3   When you look through a very powerful telescope, are you effectively looking forward or backward in time?

4   Which rogue particles stopped light from traveling around the early Universe?

5   What mysterious stuff is believed to make up more than four-fifths of the matter in the Universe?

6   Which element would not fuse with other elements in the core of stars, causing them to die?

7   What is the name given to the very hottest type of star?

8   What is the name of the first galaxy that was discovered after our own, the Milky Way?

9   What is the name of the supercluster that our galaxy, the Milky Way, is part of?

10 Why do some objects in the night sky appear reddish in color?

11 Which two strange space objects can form after a star goes supernova?

12 What name is given to tiny planets before they go on to form bigger planets?

13 Which planet in our solar system is tilted on its side?

14 What is the difference between a meteoroid and a meteor?

15 What did the ancient Greeks call comets?

16 What is an exoplanet?

17 What is "outgassing"?

18 What are the four fundamental forces?

Find the answers on page 125!

GLOSSARY

ANTENNA A dish or rod on a spacecraft or telescope used to send and receive radio signals from elsewhere.

ASTEROID An irregularly shaped rocky object, smaller than a planet, orbiting the Sun.

ATMOSPHERE The layers of gas that surround a planet, held in place by that planet's gravity. Earth's atmosphere is mostly made up of nitrogen, oxygen, carbon dioxide, water vapor and smaller amounts of other gases.

ATOM The smallest particle of a chemical element that can exist on its own.

BIG BANG THEORY The theory of how the Universe formed out of a single point around 13.8 billion years ago.

CHEMICAL ELEMENT A substance, such as hydrogen, iron, or silicon, that is made up of just one type of atom.

DARK ENERGY A yet to be seen or measured form of energy or force believed to be responsible for the expansion of the Universe.

DARK MATTER A term used by scientists to describe stuff in the Universe that cannot be seen, but is believed to exist because of its effects of gravity on other objects.

DWARF PLANET Objects such as Pluto and Ceres, which are round and orbit the Sun, but are smaller than planets.

EXTRATERRESTRIAL A being that comes from outside the Earth or its atmosphere.

GALAXY A large system of millions or billions of stars all held together by gravity. The Milky Way is our home galaxy.

GRAVITY An invisible force of attraction between objects that pulls objects toward one another and prevents things from floating off into space.

HYDROGEN The lightest chemical element with each of its atoms consisting of one electron and one proton. Hydrogen is the most common element in the Universe.

LIGHT YEAR The distance traveled by light in a year which is about 5.9 trillion miles (9.46 trillion km). This giant measure is used to describe large distances in space.

MASS The amount of stuff (scientists call it "matter") an object contains.

METEOR A meteoroid that enters a planet's atmosphere, but burns up before reaching the ground.

METEORITE A meteoroid that reaches the ground and survives impact.

METEOROID Small bits of space rock or metal that float around in space.

NASA Short for the he National Aeronautics and Space Administration, this is the USA's major space agency.

NEBULA A cloud of dust and gas in space.

NUCLEAR FUSION The reactions found in the center of the star that join the nuclei of atoms together, generating huge amounts of energy as a result.

NUCLEUS The middle part of atoms, containing neutrons and protons. It is also the term used to describe the center part of a comet.

ORBIT To travel in a circle or oval-shaped path around a planet or star. For example, Earth orbits the Sun, and the Moon orbits Earth.

OXYGEN A chemical element, naturally found as a gas, that forms 20% of Earth's atmosphere, and is vital to life.

PLANET A ball-shaped (scientists say "spherical") object that orbits a star and is large enough to have cleared its orbital path of debris.

PULSAR A small, very dense star that rotates really fast and gives out short pulses of radio waves and other electromagnetic radiation.

RADIOACTIVITY Energy that is released from unstable atoms.

SATELLITE An object that orbits another object. Satellites can be natural, such as a moon around a planet, or artificial, such as a space probe launched to orbit Earth or another object in space.

SPACE PROBE A spacecraft without a human crew launched into space to explore and send back information to Earth.

SUBATOMIC PARTICLE A particle smaller than an atom, such as an electron, neutron, or proton.

SUPERNOVA A giant, powerful explosion that tears a large star apart and scatters its matter through space.

TIDALLY LOCKED When an orbiting astronomical body such as a moon always has the same side facing the object it is orbiting.

UNIVERSE The whole of space and everything it contains, including all matter, energy, and time. In short, it's everything!

COSMIC QUIZ ANSWERS

1   The Planck Era (named after Max Planck)

2   Hydrogen

3   Backward

4   Free electrons

5   Dark matter

6   Iron

7   Type O

8   Andromeda

9   Laniakea Supercluster

10   Objects in the night sky that are moving away from us appear red, as the light they give off becomes stretched. This is called redshift.

11   Black holes or neutron stars

12   Planetesimals

13   Uranus

14   Meteoroids are small pieces of rock that travel around space. When a meteoroid enters Earth's atmosphere and burns up, it is called a meteor (also known as a shooting star).

15   "Hairy stars"

16   A planet outside of our solar system, orbiting a different star from our Sun.

17   When volcanic activity on a planet causes gases to be released from inside the planet

18   Strong nuclear force, weak nuclear force, electromagnetism, and gravity

INDEX

Inspiring | Educating | Creating | Entertaining

Brimming with creative inspiration, how-to projects, and useful information to enrich your everyday life, Quarto Knows is a favorite destination for those pursuing their interests and passions. Visit our site and dig deeper with our books into your area of interest: Quarto Creates, Quarto Cooks, Quarto Homes, Quarto Lives, Quarto Drives, Quarto Explores, Quarto Gifts, or Quarto Kids.

First published in 2020 by Wide Eyed Editions, an imprint of The Quarto Group.
100 Cummings Center, Suite 265D, Beverly, MA 01915, USA.
T +1 978-282-9590 **www.QuartoKnows.com**

A CIP record for this book is available from the Library of Congress.
ISBN 978-0-7112-6273-7
eISBN 978-0-7112-6314-7

The illustrations were created artwork created with digital media
Set in Futura

Published by Georgia Amson-Bradshaw
Designed by Myrto Dimitrakoulia
Edited by Georgia Amson-Bradshaw
Production by Dawn Cameron

Manufactured in Guangdong, China TT032022

3 5 7 9 8 6 4